SPIDERS

by Ruth Owen

BEARPORT
PUBLISHING

CREATE!

Credits

Cover, © Ruth Owen Books; 1, © Ruth Owen Books; 3, © Ruth Owen Books; 4, © Ruth Owen Books; 5, © Shutterstock; 6T, © Mirek Kijewski/Shutterstock; 6B, © Ruth Owen Books; 7, © Ruth Owen Books; 8–9, © Ruth Owen Books; 10–11, © Ruth Owen Books; 12–13, © Ruth Owen Books; 14, © Ruth Owen Books; 15T, © Shutterstock; 15B, © Ruth Owen Books; 16–17, © Ruth Owen Books; 18–19, © Ruth Owen Books; 20–21, © Ruth Owen Books; 22TL, © jax10289/Shutterstock; 22BL, © Stephen Dalton/Superstock; 22R, © Bearport Publishing; 23TL, © inewsfoto/Shutterstock; 23BL, © baibaz/Shutterstock; 23TR, © Silvia Dubois/Shutterstock; 23BR, © focal point/Shutterstock.

Photo Researcher: Ruth Owen Books with photography by Charles Francis

Library of Congress Cataloging-in-Publication Data

Names: Owen, Ruth, 1967– author.
Title: Spiders / by Ruth Owen.
Description: Create!. | Minneapolis, Minnesota : Bearport Publishing Company, 2021. | Series: Creepy crafts & more | Includes bibliographical references and index.
Identifiers: LCCN 2020006132 (print) | LCCN 2020006133 (ebook) | ISBN 9781647471897 (library binding) | ISBN 9781647471965 (ebook)
Subjects: LCSH: Handicraft—Juvenile literature. | Spiders—Juvenile literature. | Baking—Juvenile literature.
Classification: LCC TT160 .O8454 2021 (print) | LCC TT160 (ebook) | DDC 745.5—dc23
LC record available at https://lccn.loc.gov/2020006132
LC ebook record available at https://lccn.loc.gov/2020006133

For more information, write to Bearport Publishing, 5357 Penn Avenue South, Minneapolis, MN 55419. Printed in the United States of America.

Contents

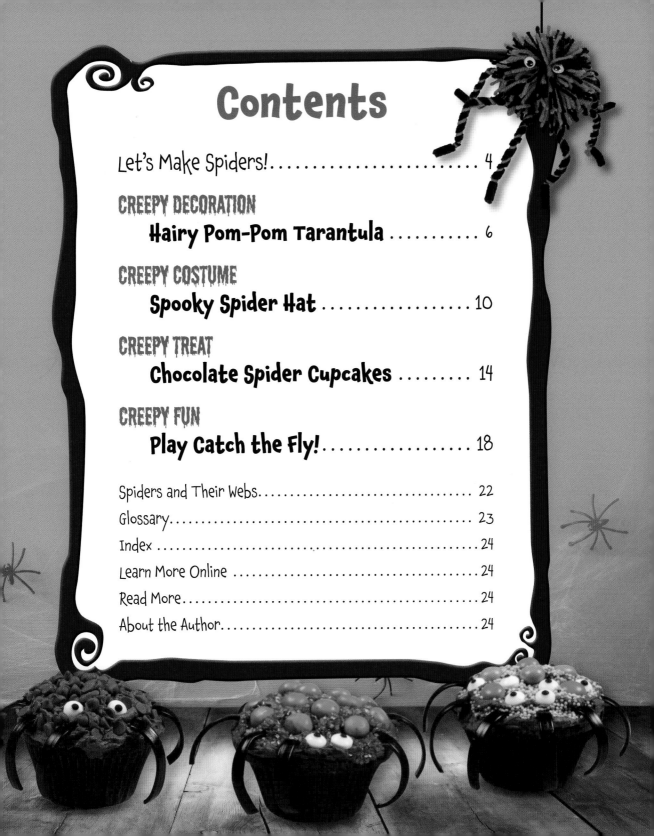

Let's Make Spiders!...................... 4

CREEPY DECORATION
Hairy Pom-Pom Tarantula 6

CREEPY COSTUME
Spooky Spider Hat 10

CREEPY TREAT
Chocolate Spider Cupcakes 14

CREEPY FUN
Play Catch the Fly!................. 18

Spiders and Their Webs.................. 22
Glossary.............................. 23
Index 24
Learn More Online 24
Read More............................ 24
About the Author....................... 24

Let's Make Spiders!

Let's get ready to make some creepy spiders! This book shows you how to make the following:

◀ A hairy pom-pom tarantula **decoration**

A fun hat that you can wear as a spidery **costume** ▶

◀ A delicious, eight-legged cupcake **treat**

A spiderweb board **game** to play with your friends ▶

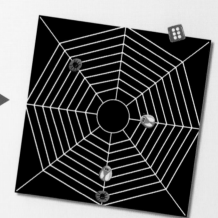

Give it a try!
If you've never done something like this before, don't be nervous. Just follow the step by step instructions and you'll soon be getting creative—and having fun!

Crafting and cooking are fantastic ways to be **creative**. But you'll enjoy this time much more if you stay safe and follow our top tips for successful creepy crafting.

Get ready to MAKE!

- Read the instructions carefully before starting. If there's anything you don't understand, ask an adult for help.

- Gather your supplies before you begin.

- Cover your work surface with old newspaper or another protective covering.

- Be careful when using sharp objects.

- When your project is complete, recycle any extra paper, cardboard, or packaging. If you have leftover materials, keep them for a future project.

- Clean up when you've finished working.

Get ready to BAKE!

- Always wash your hands with soap and hot water before you start baking.

- Make sure your work surface and supplies are clean.

- Carefully read the **recipe** before you begin. If there's a step you don't understand, ask an adult for help.

- Gather all your supplies before you start.

Measuring spoons   Measuring cups

- Carefully measure your **ingredients**. Your baking will be more successful if you use exactly the right amount.

- Ask an adult for help when using the oven.

- Clean up and put things away when you've finished baking.

Hairy Pom-Pom Tarantula

What's the biggest, hairiest spider? A tarantula! Frighten your friends with this pom-pom tarantula. Its eight striped legs are even covered in bristles.

A tarantula

YOU WILL NEED

- A ball of orange yarn
- A ball of black yarn
- Scissors
- A ruler
- A fork
- 4 black pipe cleaners that are 12 inches (30.5 cm) long
- White glue
- Googly eyes

Cut a piece of orange yarn 6 inches (15 cm) long. Thread it through the center of the fork's **tines**.

 Wrap both the orange and black yarn around the fork, working **perpendicular** to the tines.

 Make sure your piece of yarn from step 1 stays in place as you wrap the yarn about 80 times.

 Take the piece of yarn from the center of the fork's tines and tie it in a knot around the wrapped yarn.

Then, cut the loose ends of yarn to detach them from the balls.

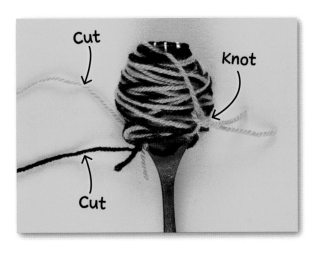

Cut

Knot

Cut

Carefully slide the bundle of yarn off the fork. Tighten the knot you just made, and then tie a second knot.

Your pom-pom should now look like this.

 Slide your scissors into two or three loops of yarn. Gently pull the loops tight and cut. Continue snipping through the loops of yarn.

 Once you've cut through all the loops, give the pom-pom a haircut to make it round.

 To make the spider's legs, cut a piece of orange yarn about 18 inches (45 cm) long. Tie the yarn to one end of a pipe cleaner. Wind the yarn around the pipe cleaner to make stripes and tie at the other end. Repeat with the other three pipe cleaners.

Overlap the four pipe cleaners to make a star shape. Then, twist them together in the center of the star.

 Bend each leg in the middle to make a knee. Add a second bend close to the end to make a foot.

 Glue the pom-pom body to the legs. Finally, glue on some googly eyes.

SCARY, EIGHT-LEGGED FUN!

Spooky Spider Hat

Love spiders? Try dressing up as one. Make a spider hat with eight eyes—just like a real spider. This hat is also a fun way to recycle because it's made of **paper-mache**, which is a material that's created from glue and newspaper!

YOU WILL NEED

- White glue
- Water
- Measuring cups
- A jar for glue mixture
- A wide paintbrush (for gluing)
- An old newspaper
- A large balloon
- A helper
- A small bowl
- Scissors
- Paintbrushes (for painting)
- Black paint
- 8 googly eyes
- Duct tape
- 8 feet (2.4 m) of black tinsel
- 8 jumbo black pipe cleaners

1. Tear the newspaper into strips about 1 inch (2.5 cm) wide.

2. Blow up the balloon so it's a little wider than your head. Ask a friend to help you check the size. Tie the end of the balloon.

3. Mix ¾ cups of white glue with ¼ cup of water in a jar. Using the wide paintbrush, brush some glue mixture over the top half of the balloon. Lay a strip of newspaper onto the glue, and then brush more glue over the top.

4. Repeat with more newspaper strips, slightly overlapping them. Keep adding strips until the top half of the balloon is completely covered.

5. Stand the balloon upright in a bowl and leave the paper-mache to dry for 24 hours. Repeat steps 3–4 to make a second layer of paper-mache. Leave to dry for 24 hours.

Dry paper-mache

Balloon

 When the paper-mache is completely dry, carefully cut off the tied end of the balloon, and slowly let the air inside escape. Remove the balloon. Use scissors to trim the bottom edge of the hat until it is even.

Put the hat on your head. If the hat covers your eyes, you can trim off a little more.

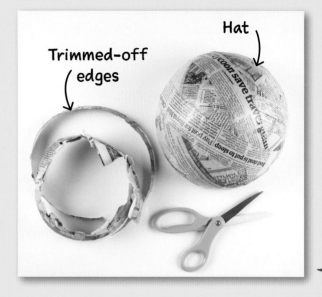

Trimmed-off edges

Hat

 Paint your hat black, and let it dry.

You may need to give your hat two coats of black paint to completely cover the newspaper.

Glue eight googly eyes onto the front of your hat. You can give your spider hat two big eyes and six smaller ones—just like a real spider.

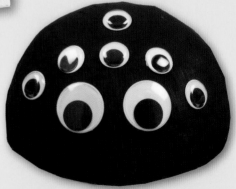

9 Cut the tinsel into eight equal pieces. Next, wind a piece of tinsel around each giant pipe cleaner. Bend the ends of the pipe cleaners back a little to hold the tinsel in place.

10 Tape four tinsel-covered pipe cleaners to the inside rim of the hat on each side. Bend the pipe cleaners so they stick out to the sides of the hat.

YOUR SPOOKY
SPIDER HAT IS READY
TO WEAR—AND
TO SCARE!

Chocolate Spider Cupcakes

Birds, frogs, lizards, and raccoons all gobble up spider snacks. And now you can, too! Don't be afraid. You don't have to eat a real spider. Just follow the steps in this recipe and you'll soon be baking a batch of 12 delicious spider cupcakes with chocolate frosting.

INGREDIENTS

To make the cupcakes:
- ½ cup cocoa powder
- 4 tablespoons hot water
- ¾ cup butter
- 1 cup granulated sugar
- 1 teaspoon baking powder
- 3 eggs
- 1 cup flour

To make the frosting:
- 4 tablespoons cocoa powder
- 2 cups powdered sugar
- ½ cup butter
- ¼ cup milk

Decorations
- 12 black licorice wheels
- Colorful sprinkles or small candies
- Candy eyes

EQUIPMENT

Measuring cups — 12-cup cupcake pan — 12 cupcake liners — 2 mixing bowls

Sieve — Oven — 2 wooden spoons — Electric mixer (or you can use a spoon)

Potholder/oven mitts — Toothpick — Butter knife — Clean scissors

 1 Preheat the oven to 400°F (200°C). Put the 12 cupcake liners into the cupcake pan.

 2 To make the cupcakes, put the cocoa powder into the mixing bowl. Carefully pour in the hot water, and mix with a wooden spoon to make a thick paste.

 3 Add the butter, sugar, baking powder, and eggs to the mixing bowl. Use a sieve to **sift** the flour into the bowl. With the electric mixer or a wooden spoon, **beat** the ingredients together until the cake **batter** is smooth and thick.

Ingredients

Batter

Spoon the mixture into the cupcake liners, dividing it equally between all 12.

Each liner will be about half filled.

 Ask an adult to carefully put the pan onto the center rack of the oven. Bake for 12 to 15 minutes. The cupcakes are done when they rise above the edges of the liners.

 Ask an adult to take the cupcake pan from the oven. Leave the cupcakes to cool completely before decorating.

To test if the cupcakes are fully baked, push a toothpick into the center of one cake and pull it back out. If the toothpick looks clean, the cupcakes are done. If there is wet cake batter on the toothpick, put the pan back into the oven for another three minutes. Then, remove and test again.

 Next, make the frosting. Put the cocoa powder, powdered sugar, and butter into a mixing bowl. Use a wooden spoon or electric mixer to beat the ingredients until well **combined**. Add milk little by little. Mix as you go until the frosting is smooth and spreadable.

To decorate, use a butter knife to spread frosting over the top of the cupcakes.

 To make the spiders' legs, unroll the licorice wheels, and use scissors to cut them into pieces 3 inches (7.5 cm) long. Then, carefully insert the closed points of the scissors into the top of a cupcake to make a small slot. Repeat seven more times. Gently push a licorice leg into each slot.

Slots

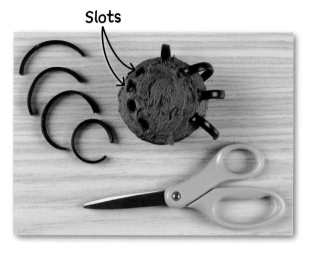

Finally, decorate each frosted cupcake with sprinkles or candies, and press on some eyes.

TIME TO EAT YOUR CREEPY TREAT!

Play Catch the Fly!

Spiders build webs of silk to catch flies and other **insects** to eat. Make your own spiderweb board game with painted stone spiders and flies. Then, have fun taking turns with friends to be either a hungry spider or a fly that must escape the spider's sticky web!

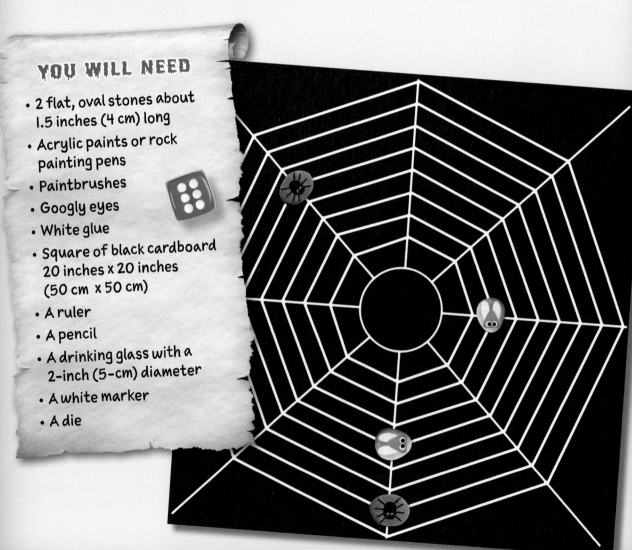

YOU WILL NEED

- 2 flat, oval stones about 1.5 inches (4 cm) long
- Acrylic paints or rock painting pens
- Paintbrushes
- Googly eyes
- White glue
- Square of black cardboard 20 inches x 20 inches (50 cm x 50 cm)
- A ruler
- A pencil
- A drinking glass with a 2-inch (5-cm) diameter
- A white marker
- A die

Gather stones to make the spider and fly playing pieces. Paint your own designs on the stones or follow the steps to the right. Complete your spider and fly by gluing on googly eyes.

How to paint a spider

 Allow the painted stones to dry.

 To make the spiderweb on the cardboard, begin by lightly drawing pencil lines diagonally across the board from corner to corner.

Place the glass over where the lines meet. Trace a circle around the glass with the white marker.

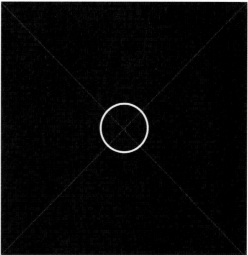

19

Using the ruler, draw four lines from the circle to the sides of the square with the marker.

 Add four more lines from the center circle to the corners of the square, similar to the spokes of a wheel.

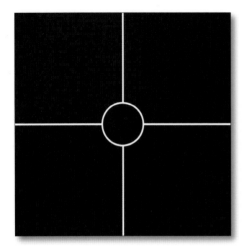

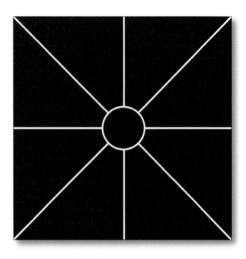

 Measure 1 inch (2.5 cm) from the center circle up one of the lines and make a pencil mark. Repeat on the next line over. Then, join the two marks using the white marker. Repeat until you've joined all eight lines.

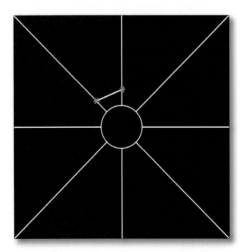

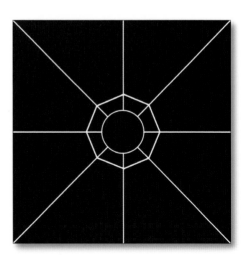

Repeat step 6 to create another set of lines 1 inch (2.5 cm) from the first.

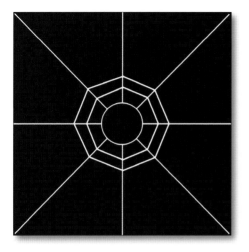

 Keep repeating step 6 until you've drawn eight sets of lines. The board is ready to play.

HOW TO PLAY CATCH THE FLY!

Set Up

Decide who will play which part. The spider starts the game at the end of a spoke along the outer edge of the web. The fly starts the game inside the center circle.

Each player rolls the die, and the highest number starts first.

How to Move

To move, the spider must roll an even number and the fly must roll an odd number. If, for example, a spider rolls a 3, they miss a turn.

Each player moves around the web at the places where the lines connect. A player can move the number of spaces of the die roll. They can go up or down a spoke or in a sideways motion around the web.

Winning

For a fly to win the game, they must roll exactly the number it would take to escape the web.

For example, if a fly rolls a 3, in order to escape, the fly's third move must be off the web.

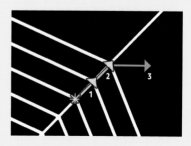

For a spider to win the game, the spider must land on a fly and capture it!

21

Spiders and Their Webs

Spiders make silk inside their **abdomens**. Orb-weaving spiders use their silk to build beautiful webs. They let out a thin thread of silk from a body part called a **spinneret**.

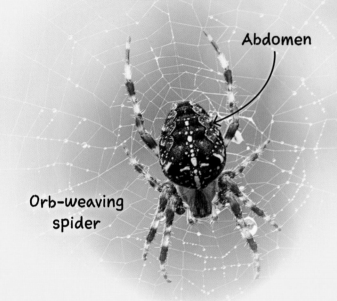

Abdomen

Orb-weaving spider

Silk

Spinneret

Building a Web

1 A spider lets out a single thread that sticks to a twig.

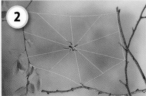

2 Next, it adds straight threads of silk that meet in the web's center.

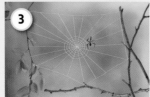

3 Then, the spider moves around the web, adding sticky strands in spirals.

4 When the web is finished, the spider hides at the edge. When an insect lands on the sticky web, the spider scurries onto the web and grabs its meal.

Glossary

abdomen the back part of a spider's body

batter dough that can be baked to make a cake

beat mix ingredients until they are smooth using a spoon, fork, whisk, or electric mixer

combined completely mixed together

ingredients the things that are used to make food

insects small animals that have six legs, three main body parts, two antennae, and a hard covering called an exoskeleton

paper-mache a material made from newspapers and glue that can be molded when it is wet and hardens as it dries

perpendicular going straight up or to the side at a 90 degree angle from another line or surface

recipe a set of instructions for making a dish or type of food

sift gently shake a loose substance, such as flour or sugar, through a sieve to remove any lumps

spinneret the body part of a spider or insect that makes and lets out silk

tines the points on a fork

Index

Catch the Fly! 4, 18–21

chocolate spider cupcakes 4, 14–17

costume 4, 10–13

ingredients 5, 14–16

orb-weaving spider 22

paper-mache 10–12

pom-pom tarantula 4, 6–9

recipe 5, 14

safety 4

spider hat 4, 10–13

tarantula 4, 6

web 4, 18–22

Read More

Camisa, Kathryn. *Hairy Tarantulas (No Backbone! Spiders).* New York: Bearport Publishing (2009).

Kenney, Karen Latchana. *Spiders (Animal Architects).* Minneapolis: Jump! (2018).

Owen, Ruth. *Make Origami Insects and Spiders (Animal Kingdom Origami).* New York: Rosen Publishing (2018).

Learn More Online

1. Go to **www.factsurfer.com**
2. Enter "**Spiders Crafts**" into the search box.
3. Click on the cover of this book to see a list of websites.

About the Author

Ruth Owen has been developing and writing children's books for more than 10 years. She lives in Cornwall, England, just minutes from the ocean. Ruth loves spiders and regularly rescues them from her three cats. As of yet, Ruth has never met a spider that was too big to pick up in her hands—even though some of the eight-legged visitors to her cottage are pretty huge and very hairy!